GETTING TO KNOW THE WORLD'S GREATEST ARTISTS

SALVADOR DALI

WRITTEN AND ILLUSTRATED BY MIKE VENEZIA

CONSULTANT MEG MOSS

℗ CHILDRENS PRESS®
CHICAGO

For my surreal son, Michael Anthony

Cover: *The Persistence of Memory*. 1931. Oil on canvas, 9 ½ x 13 inches.
Collection, The Museum of Modern Art, New York. Given anonymously.

Library of Congress Cataloging-in-Publication Data

Venezia, Mike.
  Salvador Dali / written and illustrated by Mike Venezia.
    p.   cm.–(Getting to know the world's greatest
artists)
  Summary: Briefly describes the life and work of the
twentieth-century Spanish surrealist painter, describing
and giving examples of his art.
  ISBN 0-516-02296-2
  1.   Dali, Salvador, 1904-   –Juvenile literature.
2.   Painters–Spain–Biography–Juvenile literature.
[1.   Dali, Salvador, 1904– . 2.   Artists.   3.   Painting,
Spanish.   4.   Painting, Modern–pain.   5.   Art
appreciation.]   I.   Title.   II.   Series: Venezia, Mike.
Getting to know the world's greatest artists.
ND813.D3V46 1993
759.6–dc20   92-35053
[B]   CIP
                                               AC

Saint Dali, photograph © Marc Lacroix.
Courtesy of Salvador Dali Museum, St. Petersburg, Florida.

Salvador Dali was born in Figueras, Spain, in 1904. He was one of the most famous and unusual artists of the twentieth century.

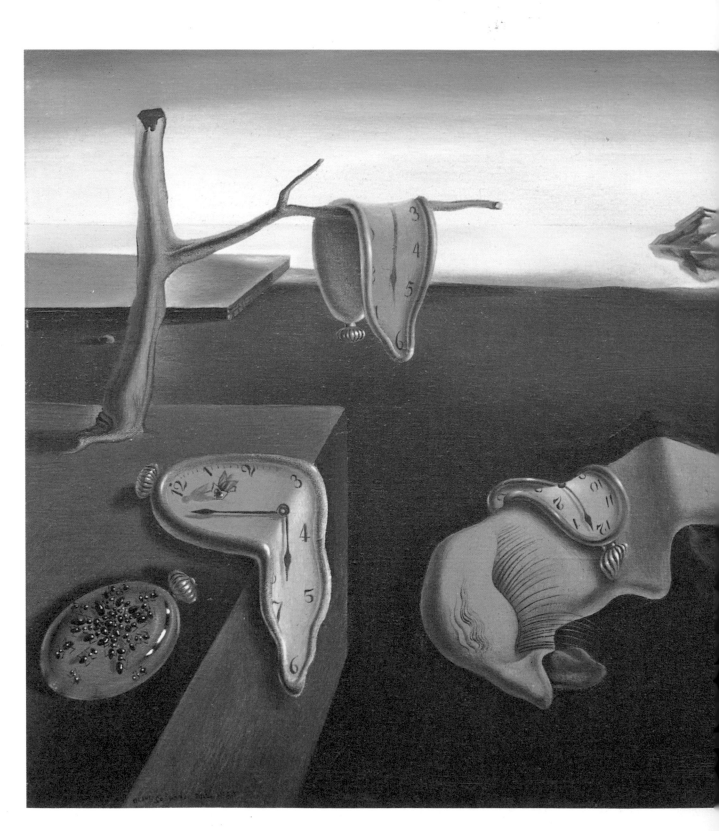

Salvador Dali's best-known paintings are called surrealistic. Most of them are filled with mysterious objects or familiar objects that have been oddly changed.

The Persistence of Memory.
1931. Oil on canvas,
9 ½ x 13 inches.
Collection, The Museum of Modern Art,
New York. Given anonymously.

Even though the things Dali painted look very real, his paintings can be hard to understand. That's because many of the scenes he chose to paint came right out of his dreams.

Metamorphosis of Narcissus.
1934. Oil on canvas,
20 1/8 x 30 3/4 inches.
Tate Gallery,
London/Art Resource, New York.

Just before Salvador Dali was born, a terrible thing happened to his mother and father. Mr. and Mrs. Dali's first son died. When their new baby arrived, they decided to name him Salvador after the child they had just lost.

They treated the new Salvador as though he were their first son, and were very protective of him.

The second Salvador was very
confused while he was growing up.

Because he was confused, Salvador
Dali acted different from other
children. He had strange dreams and
fears, and he always wanted attention.

Detail of *First Days of Spring*. c. 1929.
Oil on wood panel, 19¾ x 25⅝ inches.
Private collection. Photograph © SuperStock, New York.

Salvador Dali often showed things
in his paintings that he remembered
from his childhood, even the things
that frightened him.

Even after he grew up, Dali kept
doing things to get attention, like
arriving at an event in a limousine
filled with cauliflowers, or giving a
talk about his art while wearing a
deep-sea diving suit.

He said he received messages from outer space through his moustache, which acted like an antenna. People couldn't wait to see what Salvador Dali would come up with next.

Cadaques. 1923. Oil on canvas, 37 3/8 x 49 1/8 inches.
© Salvador Dali Museum, St. Petersburg, Florida.

While he was growing up, Salvador Dali had a wonderful imagination and was very interested in art. He may have started painting when he was only eight years old, at his family's summer home. The Dali family spent every summer in Cadaqués, Spain, which was right on the sea.

The Weaning of Furniture—Nutrition. 1934. Oil on panel, 7 x 9 ½ inches.
© Salvador Dali Museum, St. Petersburg, Florida.

Artists from all over would come
to paint the beautiful scenery there.
Some of them were friends of the
Dali family. Salvador Dali loved the
landscape around Cadaqués, and
included scenes he remembered in
many of his later paintings.

When he was a teenager, Salvador went to Madrid, the capital city of Spain, to enter its school of fine arts. Everything seemed fine at first, but soon Salvador got tired of the old-fashioned way art was being taught at the school.

He was more interested in the exciting new art being created in the city of Paris, France. Salvador Dali was especially interested in the paintings of Pablo Picasso, another Spanish artist, who lived in Paris. Dali loved the many new and modern styles of painting that Picasso invented.

Mother and Child. By Pablo Picasso. 1921. Oil on canvas, 56²/₅ x 64 inches.
© The Art Institute of Chicago. All Rights Reserved. Gift of Maymar Corporation,
Mrs. Maurice L. Rothschild, Mr. and Mrs. Chauncey McCormick;
Mary and Leigh Block Charitable Fund; Ada Turnbull Hertle Endowment;
through prior gift of Mr. and Mrs. Edwin E. Hokin, 1954.270.

Dali made many trips to Paris. On
one of his trips, he got to meet Pablo
Picasso.

Venus and Sailor.
By Salvador Dali.
1925. Oil on canvas,
84⅗ x 58 inches.
Ikeda Museum
of 20th Century Art.
Sizuoka-Ken, Japan.

Some of Dali's early works look
very much like Picasso's paintings
of that time.

Dali also became interested in a group of artists and writers in Paris known as the Surrealists.

Celebes. By Max Ernst. 1921. Oil on canvas, 49⅜ x 42½ inches. Tate Gallery, London/Art Resource, New York.

Surrealist artists such as Max Ernst, René Magritte, and Joan Miró thought up a whole new way of looking at things.

Time Transfixed. By René Magritte. 1938. Oil on canvas, 57 8/10 x 38 8/10 inches. © The Art Institute of Chicago. All Rights Reserved. Joseph Winterbotham Collection, 1970.426.

The Tilled Field. By Joan Miró, 1923-24. Oil on canvas, 26 x 36½ inches.
Solomon R. Guggenheim Museum, New York. FN 72.2020.
Photograph by David Heald, © The Solomon R. Guggenheim Foundation, New York.

They painted mostly what they remembered from their dreams, or anything that automatically popped into their minds. The Surrealists hoped their strange works of art would make people think, and discover feelings they never knew they had. They felt that stirring up thoughts from the backs of people's minds was important for artists to do.

Illumined Pleasures. 1929.
Oil and collage on composition board, 9⅜ x 13¾ inches.
Collection, The Museum of Modern Art, New York.
The Sidney and Harriet Janis Collection.

The Surrealists liked Salvador Dali, and asked him to join their group. Soon he was painting pictures filled with his own dreamlike objects.

The Surrealists thought Dali was such an interesting character that

they sometimes traveled to his home in Spain to be with him while he painted. One of the people who visited him was the wife of a Surrealist poet. Gala Eluard loved Dali's work and his unusual personality.

Gala was very imaginative, too, and liked attention as much as Dali did. Soon, they fell in love. Dali thought Gala was the most beautiful woman in the world, and used her for a model in many of his paintings, like the one on the next page. Gala helped to make sure Salvador Dali and his paintings got noticed as much as possible. Eventually, Gala divorced her husband and married Dali.

Madonna of Port Lligat. 1950.
Oil on canvas, 56 6/10 x 37 7/10 inches.
Lady James Dunn Collection, Canada.
Photograph © SuperStock, New York.

Some of Dali's most famous paintings are very tricky. He often showed that things aren't always what they appear to be at first glance. It's not clear whether the painting on the next page shows a group of people or a statue of the head of a famous French philosopher.

It's kind of like looking at clouds and imagining all the different things you can see in them.

Detail of *Slave Market With Disappearing Bust of Voltaire*. 1940.
Oil on canvas, 18¼ x 25¾ inches.
© Salvador Dali Museum, St. Petersburg, Florida.

Dali's paintings were becoming well known all over Europe and America. He wasn't afraid to show his strangest thoughts or dreams in his paintings.

Some of the Surrealists felt that Dali's dreams were too strange.

The Enigma of Hitler. 1939. Oil on canvas. 39 3/10 x 59 inches.
Museo Nacional Centro de Arte Reina Sofía, Madrid, Spain.

They were sometimes offended at what Dali showed, like the cruel dictator, Adolf Hitler, in the painting above. Dali thought this was a ridiculous thing for Surrealists to say and ended up leaving their group. He continued to paint exactly the way he wanted for the rest of his life.

Salvador Dali lived to be eighty-five years old. He is best known for his paintings, but he accomplished many other things during his life.

The Ghost of Vermeer of Delft Which Can Be Used as a Table. 1934. Oil on panel, 7 1/8 x 5 1/2 inches. © Salvador Dali Museum, St. Petersburg, Florida.

Still from the Dali film *L'Age d'or.* 1930. The Museum of Modern Art/Film Stills Archive. New York.

Dali made his own films. He was a very good writer, too. He also designed clothes, fancy perfume bottles, and ads for magazines, and he worked with famous moviemakers in Hollywood, including Walt Disney.

Salvador Dali was always surprising people with his showmanship. He is one of the few great artists who became as famous as his artwork.

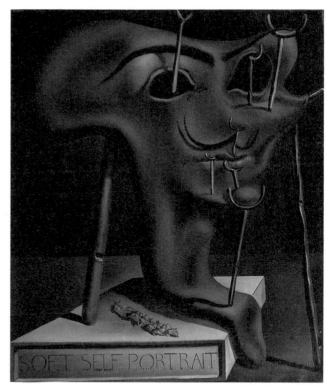

Soft Self-Portrait with Grilled Bacon.
1941. Oil on canvas, 24 ⅛ x 20 inches.
Fundació Gala-Salvador Dalí, Figueras, Spain.

Soft Construction with Boiled Beans; Premonition of Civil War. 1936.
Oil on canvas, 39 ⅜ x 39 inches.
Philadelphia Museum of Art.
The Louise and Walter Arensberg Collection.

Even though Dali showed his private thoughts in his paintings, they somehow seem familiar, and often remind people of their own private thoughts and dreams.

It's fun to see real Salvador Dali paintings close up–they look almost like photographs. Dali usually worked with tiny brushes to make his brush marks as invisible as possible.

The paintings in this book came from the museums listed below.

The Art Institute of Chicago, Chicago, Illinois
Fundacío Gala-Salvador Dalí, Figueras, Spain
Ikeda Museum of 20th Century Art, Sizuoka-Ken, Japan
Museo Nacional Centro de Arte Reina Sofía, Madrid, Spain
The Museum of Modern Art, New York, New York
Philadelphia Museum of Art, Philadelphia, Pennsylvania
Salvador Dali Museum, St. Petersburg, Florida
The Solomon R. Guggenheim Museum, New York, New York
Tate Gallery, London, England